CROWDED HOUSE
WOODFACE

GW00642730

Folio © 1994 International Music Publications Limited
Southend Road · Woodford Green · Essex IG8 8HN
Music Transcribed by Barnes Music Engraving Limited, East Sussex TN22 4HA
Cover Art by Nick Seymour
Inlay Photograph by Denis Keeley

Printed by Panda Press · Haverhill · Suffolk CB9 8PR
Binding by ABS · Cambridge

215-2-989

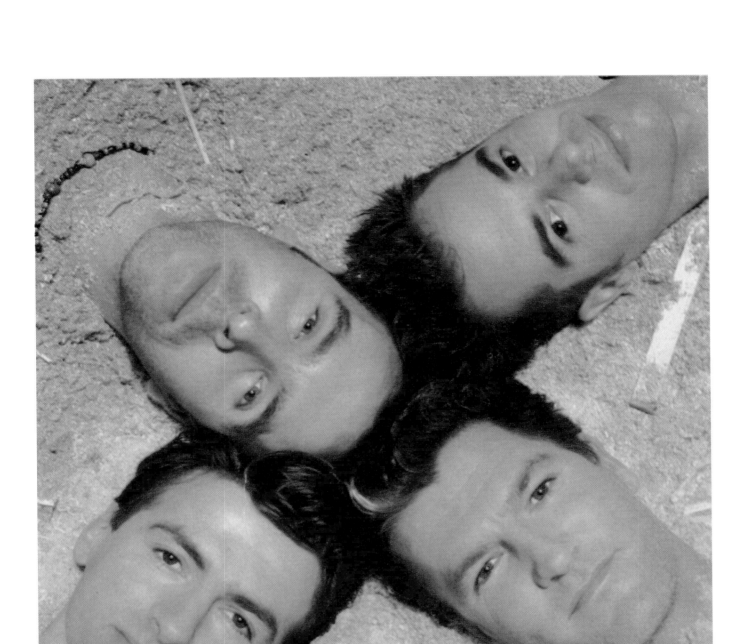

CHOCOLATE CAKE

Words & Music by
Neil Finn & Tim Finn

IT'S ONLY NATURAL

Words & Music by
Neil Finn & Tim Finn

FALL AT YOUR FEET

Words & Music by
Neil Finn

Lyrics:
1. I'm real-ly close to-night

and I feel__ like I'm mov-ing in - side__ her,
there's some-thing in__ the way__ that you're talk-ing,

ly - ing in__ the dark_____
words don't sound__ right,

and I think that I'm__ be-gin -
but I hear them__ all

TALL TREES

Words & Music by
Neil Finn & Tim Finn

1. Watch out big ships are wait - ing, salt fro - zen on your cheek,
2. Sun sleeps on mist - y morn - ing, light years from chan - nel three,

I saw a girl and boy ar - riv - ing and a steam - er put out to sea.___ Tall tree
I feel___ half - way to ze - ro, call me a he - ro, I might just a - gree.

WEATHER WITH YOU

Words & Music by
Neil Finn & Tim Finn

1. Walk-ing 'round the room sing-ing Storm - y Wea - ther at Fif-ty-

- Sev - en Mount Plea-sant Street.___ Well it's the same room but ev-ery-thing's dif-

2. Well, there's a

small boat made of chi - na, it's go-ing no-where on the man-tle - piece,___ well, do I

lie like a lounge-room liz - ard or do I sing like a bird re-leased.___ Ev-ery-where you go

al-ways take the wea - ther with you, ev-ery-where you go___ al-ways take the wea -

WHISPERS AND MOANS

Words & Music by
Neil Finn

FOUR SEASONS IN ONE DAY

Words & Music by
Neil Finn & Tim Finn

1. Four_ sea-sons in one day_____ ly-ing in the depths_ of your i-ma-gi-na-tion,
2. Smil-ing as the shit comes down,_____ you can tell a man_ from what he has_ to say._____

worlds a-bove and worlds be-low,_____ the sun shines on the black clouds hang-ing o-ver the_ do-
Ev-ery-thing gets turned a-round_____ and I will risk my neck a-gain, a-gain_____

-main. Ev-en when you're feel-ing_ warm,_____ the
you can take me where you_ will_____

It does-n't pay_ to make pre-dic-tions, sleep-ing on_ an un-made bed,_ find-ing out wher-

-ev-er there is com-fort there is_____ pain on-ly one step a - way,_____ like

D.% al Coda

⊕ *CODA*

four sea-sons in one day._____

four sea-sons in one_ day.____

THERE GOES GOD

Words & Music by
Neil Finn & Tim Finn

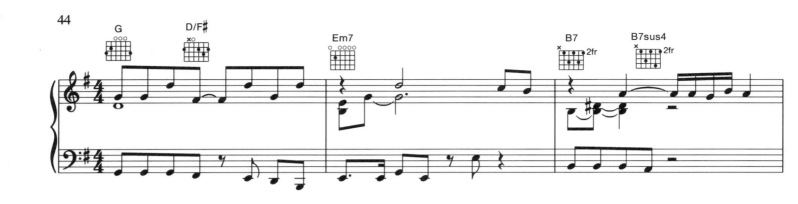

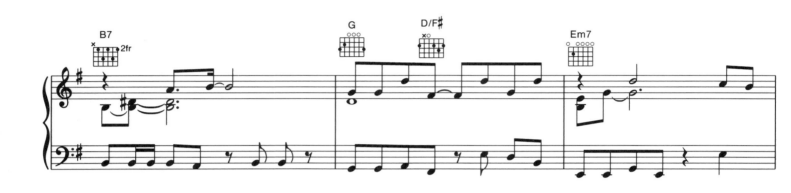

There goes   God,___   there goes   God.___

FAME IS

Words & Music by
Neil Finn

1. Fork light - ning in___
2. Now the rest of us are liv -

___ your hall,___ break the skin when you break the___ fall,___
-ing in a daze,___ keep think-in' 'bout the choice to be made.

I'll be the one___ to fix it up.___
Here come the hand - maid-ens of end time,___

1st time only

ALL I ASK

Words & Music by
Neil Finn & Tim Finn

AS SURE AS I AM

Words & Music by
Neil Finn

Don't_____ wan - na be__ there, don't_____ wan - na be__ spared._____ I'll wear the smile__ on_ your_ face,__ I am____ as sure___ as I___ am_

ITALIAN PLASTIC

Words & Music by
Paul Hester

64

Who ya gon-na take to the ball to - night? Who ya gon-na take to the dance to - night?

Who ya gon-na take to the dance to - night? Who ya gon-na take to the dance to - night, to - night,

repeat to fade

to - night? to - night?

SHE GOES ON

Words & Music by
Neil Finn

(♩ = 114)
Amaj9 Aadd9 Amaj9 Aadd9 B
2fr
Bsus4 Amaj9 Aadd9 Amaj9 Aadd9
2fr
E Esus4 E
1. Pret - ty soon you'll be a - ble to re-mem - ber her
owe it all to Frank Si - na - tra the song was
Amaj7
ly - ing in the gar - den sing - ing,
play - ing as she walked in - to the room.

In her soft_____ wind I_____ will whis-

HOW WILL YOU GO

Words & Music by
Neil Finn & Tim Finn

Printed in England
Panda Press · Haverhill · Suffolk • 1/95